Games Around the World

Yo-Yo Tricks

by Cynthia Klingel and Robert B. Noyed

Content Adviser: John Stangle, President of the American Yo-Yo Association, 1997 Advanced Division World Yo-Yo Champion
Social Science Adviser: Professor Sherry L. Field, Department of Curriculum and Instruction, College of Education, The University of Texas at Austin
Reading Adviser: Dr. Linda D. Labbo, Department of Reading Education, College of Education, The University of Georgia

COMPASS POINT BOOKS

MINNEAPOLIS, MINNESOTA

Compass Point Books
3722 West 50th Street, #115
Minneapolis, MN 55410

Visit Compass Point Books on the Internet at *www.compasspointbooks.com* or e-mail your request to
custserv@compasspointbooks.com

Photographs ©: Gregg Andersen, cover, 2, 5, 10, 11, 12, 14, 29; Roger
Ressmeyer/Corbis, 4; Victoria & Albert Museum, London/Art Resource, N.Y., 6;
Giraudon/Art Resource, N.Y., 7; Caroline Penn/Corbis, 9; James A. Sugar/Corbis, 26.

Editors: E. Russell Primm and Emily J. Dolbear
Photo Researchers: Svetlana Zhurkina and Jo Miller
Photo Selector: Emily J. Dolbear
Designer: Bradfordesign, Inc.
Illustrator: Brandon Reibeling

Library of Congress Cataloging-in-Publication Data

Klingel, Cynthia Fitterer.
    Yo-yo tricks / by Cynthia Klingel and Robert Noyed.
        p. cm. — (Games around the world)
    Includes bibliographical references and index.
    Summary: Presents a history of yo-yos and yo-yo tricks, along with
    tips and easy step-by-step instructions for performing several tricks.
    ISBN 0-7565-0193-8 (hardcover)
        1. Yo-yos—Juvenile literature. [1. Yo-yos.] I. Noyed, Robert B. II. Title. III. Series.
    GV1216 .K55 2002
    796.2—dc21   2001004732

Table of Contents

What Is a Return Top?

What is a return top? What is a spin-
ner? What do you need to **walk** the
dog? What do you use to go around
the world? Can you guess? The answer
is—a **yo-yo!**

▲ *A yo-yo*

   A yo-yo is a spinning toy on a
string. The string is used to make the
yo-yo spin. People once called the
yo-yo a spinning top. It looks like a top
as it spins up and down on the string.

   It is fun to play with a yo-yo. It is also exciting to watch people do
tricks with yo-yos. Let's learn more about the yo-yo. Then we'll learn
how to do some yo-yo tricks.

The History of Yo-Yos

The yo-yo is a very old toy. It is believed to be the second-oldest toy in history. (The doll is the oldest toy.)

The yo-yo was first seen in Greece more than 2,500 years ago. It was called a disk. The Greeks painted colorful pictures on the clay disks.

The yo-yo was also a popular toy in the Philippines. Children in the Philippines still play with yo-yos.

In the 1700s, the yo-yo was popular in England. It was called a bandalore. The bandalore was an adult toy. Kings and many other wealthy people played with bandalores.

▲ In this painting from the 1700s, a young boy believed to be the French king Louis XVII plays with a yo-yo.

◄ A woman plays with a yo-yo in this Indian watercolor from about 1725.

7

In France, the yo-yo was called *l'émigrette*. In the 1800s, people in France formed "joujou" clubs. *Joujou* is another name for yo-yo.

In the 1860s, when bandalores came to the United States, people called yo-yos return wheels. In the 1920s, a man from the Philippines named Pedro Flores brought a yo-yo to the United States. Flores started a company that made yo-yos in California in 1928.

Soon a man named Donald Duncan bought this company. He began making the famous Duncan yo-yos in 1930. Duncan held yo-yo demonstrations and contests across the United States. People all over the world, including Australia, Great Britain, and Japan, still perform yo-yo tricks today.

An Inupiat Eskimo woman makes traditional yo-yos from sealskin. ▶

Yo-Yo Trick Basics

When you buy a yo-yo, shop at a store that lets you try out different yo-yos. That way you can find the one that works best for you. Your first yo-yo does not have to be expensive. Very old and unusual yo-yos can cost hundreds of dollars!

The yo-yo is a simple toy, so it is easy to learn its parts. It usually has two round, flat pieces of wood or plastic joined at the center by a peg, or **axle**. A long string is attached to the axle.

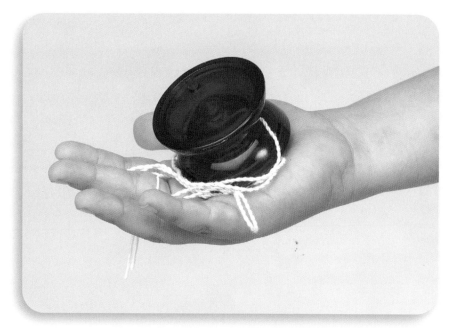

▲ *A long string attaches to a peg at the center of the yo-yo.*

On the free end of the string is a loop. You don't use this loop to make the yo-yo move. Instead, you make a **slipknot** by putting a section of the string through the loop. This new loop is where you put the middle finger of your yo-yo hand—your **string finger**.

At this point, you have to check the length of the string. First, put your hand level with your belly button and let your yo-yo fall. The yo-yo should just touch the floor.

▲ *Can you tell that this yo-yo string is way too long?*

11

A yo-yo can last a long time. Sometimes the string begins to wear out. A worn-out string makes it harder to do tricks. So if this happens, you must change the string.

Holding the yo-yo properly is easy. With the loop around your string finger, cup the yo-yo in the palm of your hand. The yo-yo should be resting with the string coming from your finger, over the top of the yo-yo, and around the yo-yo.

▲ Loop the yo-yo string around your middle finger.

Once you are holding your yo-yo correctly, you are ready to start. Before you try to do tricks though, you need to learn the throws. Every yo-yo trick requires one of the throws—and the throws take practice. They sometimes feel like tricks themselves.

How Big Is the Biggest Yo-Yo in the World?

Can you guess? It weighs 256 pounds (116 kilograms)! It stands 50 inches (127 centimeters) tall. You can have your picture taken next to this giant yo-yo at the National Yo-Yo Museum in Chico, California. Other yo-yos and related objects up to eighty years old are also on display.

You can throw a yo-yo in several different ways. The easiest throw is called the Gravity Pull. Another throw is the Basic Power Throw. Then there's the Forward Pass and the Sleeper. Remember, practice makes perfect!

◀ *There are many tricks to learn.*

Gravity Pull

Setup: Stretch your arm straight out in front of you. Hold the yo-yo in your hand, with your palm facing the floor.

How to throw:

1. Let go of the yo-yo. Let your hand move downward as the string of the yo-yo unwinds.

2. Just before the yo-yo gets to the end of its string, raise your hand. This will bring the yo-yo back to your hand.

3. When the yo-yo gets back to your palm, catch it!

▲ Gravity Pull

Basic Power Throw

Setup: Stretch your arm straight out in front of you. Hold the yo-yo in your hand, with your palm facing the ceiling. Keeping your arm out in front of you, bend your elbow until your hand is in front of your eyes.

How to throw:

1. Throw your arm forward. This will make the yo-yo roll forward, off your fingers.

▲ *Basic Power Throw*

2. Turn your hand over. Lift your string finger. This will make the yo-yo come back to you!

16

Forward Pass

Setup: Let your arm hang at your side. Hold the yo-yo loosely in your hand, with your palm facing behind you.

How to throw:

1. Swing your arm back and then forward.

2. As your arm is swinging forward, turn your palm to face forward. Let the yo-yo fly forward.

3. Remember to bend your elbow so that it stays next to your body.

4. After the yo-yo unwinds, it will return to your hand. Be ready!

▲ Forward Pass

The Sleeper

The Sleeper is like the Basic Power Throw without the tug when the yo-yo unwinds. Then, the yo-yo spins in its loop at the end of the string.

Setup: Stretch your arm straight out in front of you. Hold the yo-yo in your hand, with your palm facing the ceiling. Keeping your arm out in front of you, bend your elbow until your hand is in front of your eyes.

How to throw:

1. Throw your arm forward. Let the yo-yo roll forward, off your fingers, toward the floor.

▲ *The Sleeper*

2. Your yo-yo will be spinning at the bottom of the string. Your yo-yo is **sleeping**.

3. When you want your yo-yo to come back, turn your palm down and lift your string finger.

4. Remember, the more powerful your throw, the longer the yo-yo will sleep and the faster it will spin.

Rock the Baby

Now you are ready for some tricks. Can you Rock the Baby?

Setup: Follow directions for throwing a sleeper. For this trick, it needs to be a long sleeper.

How to do the trick:

1. Once the yo-yo is sleeping, raise your hand. Spread your fingers apart as if you are signaling someone to stop. Now your string finger will be pointing to the ceiling.

▲ Take the string between your thumb and forefinger.

2. With your other hand, take the yo-yo string between your thumb and the finger next to your thumb.

20

3. Pull the string over your thumb.

4. As you pull it, move your fingers between the strings. You are making a space for the yo-yo to swing through.

5. Stop pulling when there is enough room for the yo-yo to swing between the strings.

6. Move your yo-yo hand back and forth gently until the yo-yo swings through the "cradle."

▲ *Then you'll be Rocking the Baby!*

7. When you are finished, let go of the yo-yo with your free hand. The yo-yo will return to your other hand.

Walk the Dog

This trick is often included in contests. How far can you Walk the Dog?

Setup: Throw a sleeper. Fast sleepers work better for this trick.

How to do the trick:

1. When the yo-yo begins to sleep, lower your arm so that the yo-yo just touches the ground.

2. Move your hand forward. The yo-yo will move forward, or "walk," as it spins.

▲ *Walking the Dog*

3.	After you have walked your yo-yo several inches, lift your hand.

4.	When you tug on the string, the yo-yo will return to your hand!

How Many Yo-Yos?

Most tricks require only one yo-yo. With practice, you can do tricks with two, three, or even four yo-yos! In time, you could Walk the Dog with a yo-yo in each hand!

Around the World

This famous trick requires a very good Sleeper and Forward Pass. The yo-yo swings around in big circles, so practice in a safe place with plenty of room.

Setup: Follow directions for the Forward Pass. Let the yo-yo go up toward the ceiling.

How to do the trick:

1. Let the yo-yo reach the end of the string. Then, instead of yanking it back into your hand, gently make it sleep.

▲ *Make sure to tell your friends to stand back.*

2. Your wrist should turn, keeping the yo-yo moving in a large circle.

3. When the yo-yo has made a full circle and is back in front of you, tug gently on the string. The yo-yo will return to your hand.

4. After lots of prac- tice, try swinging the yo-yo in two circles before making it return to your hand.

▲ *Going Around the World*

Playing with Yo-Yos

Yo-yos come in many colors. They may be made of plastic, aluminum, or wood. Some yo-yos are shiny and they glow when they spin. Most yo-yos are round, but some yo-yos are made in different shapes. All yo-yos have a string!

Playing with yo-yos is so much fun. Learning how to make a yo-yo move up and down can take some time. Once you learn how to do that, though, you can try some of the tricks.

When you know how to do a few yo-yo tricks, keep practicing. You will soon be able to do the tricks very well. Then you can entertain your friends and family with a Walk the Dog trick or even an Around the World.

◀ *A floating astronaut plays with a yo-yo during a training flight.*

Glossary

axle—the peg that holds the two parts of a yo-yo together

sleeping—a yo-yo spinning at the bottom of the string is said to be "sleeping"

slipknot—a knot that slips along the string around which it is made

string finger—the middle finger of the hand used to do yo-yo tricks

walk—to move the yo-yo forward

yo-yo—a small toy made up of a string wound around two round, flat pieces joined at the center by a peg. The player loops the string around the string finger and spins the yo-yo up and down on the string.

Did You Know?

- Luck, Wisconsin, became the "yo-yo capital of the world" when the Duncan Yo-Yo Company moved there in 1946. The company made 3,600 yo-yos per hour!

- Astronauts brought yo-yos into space on the space shuttle *Discovery* in 1985 and on the *Atlantis* in 1992. They used yo-yos to study gravity.

- More than half a billion yo-yos have been sold in the United States since 1930.

- June 6 is National Yo-Yo Day in the United States. This day honors Donald Duncan's birthday.

Want to Know More?

At the Library

Cassidy, John. *The Klutz Yo-Yo Book*. Palo Alto, Calif.: Klutz, Inc., 1998.

Roper, Ingrid. *Yo-Yos: Tricks to Amaze Your Friends.* New York: HarperCollins Juvenile Books, 2001.

Sayco, Larry. *The Ultimate Yo-Yo Book: 20 Great Tricks and Tips!* New York: Grosset & Dunlap, 1998.

Weber, Bruce. *Advanced Yo-Yo Tricks.* New York: Cartwheel Books, 1999.

On the Web

The American Yo-Yo Association, Inc.

http://www.ayya.net/

For upcoming yo-yo events, results of past events, rules, and yo-yo tricks

Duncan Yo-Yo

http://www.yo-yo.com

For yo-yo history and photographs

Yo-Yo Clubs

http://www.ayya.net/club.html

For a yo-yo club near you

Through the Mail

The American Yo-Yo Association, Inc.

12106 Fruitwood Drive

Riverview, FL 33569

To get information about becoming a member

On the Road

The National Yo-Yo Museum

320 Broadway

Chico, CA 95928

916/893-0545

To see a dazzling display of more than 1,000 yo-yos

Index

About the Authors

Cynthia Klingel has worked as a high school English teacher and an elementary school teacher. She is currently the curriculum director for a Minnesota school district. Cynthia Klingel lives with her family in Mankato, Minnesota.

Robert B. Noyed started his career as a newspaper reporter. Since then, he has worked in school communications and public relations at the state and national level. Robert B. Noyed lives with his family in Brooklyn Center, Minnesota.